Starting and Buying Businesses to Becoming a Seasoned Dealmaker

My Professional Journey

Arturo Henriquez

This book is dedicated to my Family!

I am forever grateful to my mother and father who opened the doors of opportunity and taught me the most valuable lesson of all: To have a deep sense of personal responsibility. I am grateful to my loving wife and my two lovely daughters who constantly inspire me to be a better man. And I am grateful to my brothers and sister for their unconditional love and support.

I am who I am because of all of you!

Table of contents

Introduction

Anybody can buy a small business with little or no experience and in most cases without using any of their money or, better yet, using somebody else's money. While this sounds like it is easier said than done, you'd be surprised how many times there are multiple million dollar businesses that are purchased without using one's own capital and by people that do not have experience in the same industry. This a day in day out reality. There is vast availability of debt and equity in the market from either institutions or private lenders or financiers or equity holders or the owners themselves. The deals we have structured have an outsider financier component for the majority of the purchase price. And we have done many successful deals without our cash or equity at stake. But, essentially, anybody is really one deal away from buying a business and completely transforming their life.

Most people think buying a business is an insurmountable event. It is something that is beyond their reach. How do you run a business? How do you understand the financials? Where do I get the money to buy this business? How do I deal with employees? How do I deal with suppliers? Can I really do this? I don't know anything about the product or the service? I don't know anything about the industry? Where do I start? These and thousands of other questions usually prevent most people from going out and buying a business. The irony is that buying a business is not that difficult. And I would venture to say it is easy when properly guided. All these doubts and concerns are in people's minds and prevent them from trying, from venturing. It really is not that hard. I have done this for over 25 years. And the truth is, whether you buy a restaurant, a distribution company, a technology company, a dry cleaner, a gym, or pretty much any small business, there are common denominators in every business that I purchased that can be easily learned by anybody. Business fundamentals and learning how to buy a business all share the same guidelines. Followed correctly, anyone can buy a business. You are really only ONE deal away from completely transforming your life.

Buying a business is a life altering event. You are no longer bound to a corporate job. You are your own boss. You are able to guide your own life. You obtain financial freedom, professional independence, stature and more importantly, you begin to create wealth. Done properly, buying a business is very easy to do. It is no different than buying a home. And most people buy one home in their lifetime, if not multiple homes. Obviously, there needs to be tenacity and hard work is required. There is detail and there is knowledge to be learned. There is experience to be obtained.

So let me talk a little bit about myself and my over 25-year journey in deal making. I have been an entrepreneur for over 25 years. I'm 47 years old as of the writing this book and have been involved in well over 130 business purchases and business deals.

I have successfully started, bought and or sold over 45 companies personally for my own portfolio. In some cases, I have had partners, mostly operating partners. I have bought many restaurants, started a tequila company, a consumer goods export company, a technology company, I have bought bars and night clubs, a pest control company, fast food restaurants, real estate brokerages, a steel fabrication company, franchises, wholesale distributers, a NAP, a loan servicing company, a logistics company, an import and distributor of electrical appliances, an oil and gas company, a theatre production, a professional soccer game, a senior living management company, among others. These have all been done by me for my own portfolio.

I have raised money from friends and families. I have raised money from venture capital funds like Merrill Lynch Venture Capital, CVC Latin America which is Citibank's venture capital arm as well as Explorador fund in Silicon Valley. I've taken a company public on the stock market in the United States, what is commonly known as an IPO or initial public offering. And I have done corporate takeovers as an entrepreneur. And I have raised millions of dollars from banks, asset based lending institutions and angel investors. All of this for my portfolio companies previously mentioned.

In addition to the businesses I have bought and sold, I have also been involved in over 30 deals or transactions where I risked my own capital. These are somewhat different than buying a business, yet obey in most part the general guidelines of buying company's. I also have been involved in sweat equity startups.

I have worked in Wall Street and other mergers and acquisitions and financial institutions over the past 25 years where I participated in over 60 transactions that were directly involved in the buying and selling of businesses. I've worked for the likes of Bank of America, Goldman Sachs, Lehman Brothers, this is the Lehman Brothers long before it dissolved and went into bankruptcy in fact over 10 years before that, back in 1999 when Lehman Brothers was the lean mean fighting machine on Wall Street. I've worked as managing director at KPMG where I spearheaded their mergers and acquisition department from start up to multiple deals a year in pipeline. In the corporate world I have sold companies (divestitures). I've bought business. I've helped companies raise funds via private equity. I have restructured companies. I have divested parts of companies. I was involved in valuations, financial advisories, due diligences, and financial and operational restructurings.

I also want to point out that I have invested in my education and I cannot stress enough how important this is. Investment in one's education is probably the single best investment that my family made in me and that I then made in myself and I continue to make in myself to this day. There is no substitute for learning best practices. I have three Master's degrees (Post-graduate), a Master's in Business Administration (MBA) Kellogg Graduate School of Management at Northwestern University and a double Master's in International Relations and Communications from Boston University. There is no substitute for learning how to do things differently. There is no substitute for creativity. Having practical, hands on experience in real life I believe needs to be balanced with theory. Just plain life experience I believe is not enough. If you're out there hustling, you're out their deal making and you're so involved in your own everyday businesses, it's hard to take a step back and gain perspective. It is hard to take a step back and see what else you're missing. Questions like what else can I apply to this business? What else can I apply to my Deal making Strategies? What am I missing? What are the new funding source? What are the new technologies that are out there? What does the new marketing and advertising look like? What are the best practices today? Where is this industry heading in 5, 10 even 20 years and what is driving these changes? Ten years ago online advertising wasn't even on the horizon. Today, it's hard to survive without having an online presence let alone proactive online marketing and advertising strategies. And this is no longer new, yet I know most small businesses are not employing this because that have not taken the time to learn and reeducate themselves about their business and everything that affects it. By education, I don't mean go out and get a graduate degree. I mean always have one foot in education, in theory, in academia. There are online courses. There are many local educational programs. And yes, to those that see the value, there are undergraduate and graduate programs and diplomas. You will be more enriched and you will have that ever so important balance between theory and real life experiences. Having both makes for a lethal preparation for really anything that you do not just professional but personal. Trust Me.

So all in all at the age of 47, as an entrepreneur, financier, private equity and professional, have been involved in well over 130 businesses and business deals. And I have done deals of all shapes, sizes and colors. So a very long curriculum in my background with regards to buying businesses. So needless to say I've been around the block a couple of time and seen pretty much everything. To use a famous quote, "I know a thing or two about a thing or two" when it comes to buying businesses, deal making and anything surrounding it.

My Professional Journey

Here is my professional journey in a somewhat chronological order so you can better understand how various elements of my life have led me to become a successful and true dealmaker and a business acquirer. I have lived both in the United States and in Mexico. I was born in Mexico but from the age of 5 we moved to the United States. I was afforded a very good education in New England. I went to private schools from Elementary through High School. I went to Boston University and majored in Economics with a double minor in Business Administration and Psychology. I graduated from Boston University when I was 21 years old and I was recruited into a management trainee program for an asset based lending company out of Dallas, TX named Associates First Capital Corporation. This is where I started my professional career, my professionally "paid" career that is.

Prior to this I had done some internships. I worked at Smith Barney, a retail stock broker, where I was cold calling clients on a daily basis. Now, I wasn't getting paid but I was learning how to build a business and I was understanding what sales was and how hard it is and how important it is and how important it is to master the sale and master what is prospecting and lead generation. Of course, I didn't master it back then but it gave me a glimpse into what these financial retail brokers had to do on a day to day to day basis to build their businesses. It was very hard work and if you were not persistent and did not have a long term stomach for it, you would not make it. I also worked briefly in a mining company in the middle of nowhere in Oaxaca, Mexico. I obtained deep respect to the hardworking blue collar employees in these mines. They are in the middle of nowhere with very little resources and infrastructure. They spend all day every day in a mine where it's very, very hot. The climate is extremely difficult. It's dry. There are no lights where they live. And there's no cities or towns around them. They basically work in the mine all day, they eat and go to sleep and they repeat this day in and day out. So it is a very desolate life. And so you get to appreciate how hard these people work to feed their families and to make a living.

But my first paying job was at Associates First Capital Corporation. Associates was an asset based lending corporation specifically in equipment financing with a focus on the transportation, construction and telecommunications industries, although they had other products. I was lucky enough to have been accepted into their management trainee program. The management training program was a fast track program where they take a couple of students fresh out of University and teach them the basics of how to run a business, how to run the asset based lending business. They sent us to a local/regional branch that was essentially self-sufficient and ran like a small business. I was sent from Boston to a branch outside of Seattle, Washington. The program entailed training in all departments of the branch for several months at any one department. I started at the sales division. Here the sales people are going out to all the dealerships that are selling equipment and offering them financing and retail financing for them and programs for their retail clients whom are buying John Deere or Caterpillar equipment or whatever equipment brand was being sold by the dealership.

I was able to see how they dealt with clients, how they prospect a new client, how they kept existing clients happy, and the constant internal struggle between them and another department within the same organization, the credit department. Once they brought in a prospective client, the credit department had to approve the loan or the financing package. Whereas sales people's focus is to sell, the credit department's focus is to manage risk. And so there's a natural conflict there because the salesperson obviously thinks every client is credit worthy and the credit department plays devil's advocate so to speak or is skeptical. This makes for a healthy loan approval process with proper checks and balances. I was rotated through the sales department for a couple of weeks. Then I went to the credit department and saw the flip side of process. I observed how they received the sales package for these new prospects, how to analyze the financial statements, the history of the company, the products and services, how the loan was going to be collateralized, the paperwork needed among many other aspects. It was certainly risk management, a strong contrast to selling. I gained two very different perspectives for essentially one goal which is to finance a client. It was eye opening indeed. From there I went over to collections department. This department makes sure that all the clients that have been funded and have a loan are paying on time. And of course not all clients are always paying on time. And sometimes some clients don't pay at all. They may fall into distress and stop paying their loans.

In the collections department they are constantly calling the clients, trying to work with these clients and trying to come up with solutions. And in many cases they're having to deal with lawyers to start litigation so that they can try to recover the loan because the client simply cannot or will not pay. And so again, I was exposed to another facet of the company that has a very different perspective on clients then the other two departments I had been in. It is funny how these perspectives are so different when dealing with the exact product. At sales everyone is happy. Sale people are selling and collecting commissions. In the credit department, clients are being approved and receiving loans. The clients were happy. Associates First Capital was happy with the new business. But to be in the Collections department is to see the dark side of lending business. The clients are in distress. And of course Associates First Capital is worried and in many cases losing money. Everyone is unhappy. Really, two very different sides of the same coin.

Then I went to a more neutral department which is the Operations Department. This is the day to day operations of the business. This is where you process payments, you send invoices, you deal with files, you deal with prospecting, and you manage the employees within the branch. In this department you experience the full operation as you are dealing with the different clients, different suppliers, the corporate office, other branches, hiring new employees, and dealing with firing or letting other employees go. So, really, the nitty gritty and ins and outs of running a business.

The last department I was exposed to in the Management Training Program was the management department with the Branch Manager. This is where it got really interesting because up to this point, I had been around all the different departments and understood how to run a business from within, I was in the business. But I was ultimately in training to how to operate the whole, and not the pieces. I got to finally see the strategic side of the business. How to set goals. How to set objectives and how to motivate people to meet those objectives. How to bring out the best in people that have talents and skills. How to turn a mediocre employee who has potential to become a great employee? And ultimately leading the dynamics and culture of this ship, this branch, into profitability day in and day out. Making sure that the dynamic is in place and the environment has the correct culture to make these five very different departments really operate in sync, operate like a smooth machine, operate like a fine tuned orchestra. That is hard work and that's what the manager has to do.

The manager has to make sure that the sales and the credit people aren't killing themselves. That they're exist a smooth communication with collections. I know people have different motivators and agendas. It is ultimately the manager's role in making sure that all of these different conflicting forces and attitudes and mindsets and different objectives all are aligned to the bigger objective. And that the common objective is making the business profitable and hitting those revenue and profitability targets for the branch so that that branch in turn makes money for corporate and corporate then in turn makes money for their shareholders. I got to see all departments albeit at a smaller level because I was at a branch and not at the corporate level so to speak. And so it was extremely enriching. So certainly it was a very interesting experience in my first "paying" job. It was an ideal job for a newly minted freshly out of college kid like myself that had really never worked o truly understood what went into making a business run and run well. So that was my first job.

From Seattle we went on to conquer Mexico. Mexico had just signed NAFTA, the North American Free Trade Agreement, with the United States and Canada. And a part of NAFTA was allowing financial institutions to work and compete head to head with Mexican banks and Mexican financial institutions in Mexico. Many financial institutions were doing the same thing Associates First Capital was, establishing a direct presence. Bank of America, Citibank, JP Morgan among many others all had representative offices in Mexico but they could not lend locally. Now they could. And so they were strengthening and expanding their local operations. And many other financial institutions, commercial banks, investment banks, asset based lending banks, credit cards institutions were now, through NAFTA, coming to Mexico. It was a very interesting time in Mexico.

So, in hindsight, I realized why Associates First Capital may had hired me. I spoke English and Spanish and understood the dual cultures of the United States and Mexico. They had the intention of establishing an operation in Mexico and going after the Mexican corporate clients just as they were doing in the United States and elsewhere in the world. So as part of this endeavor, I got to see, partake and start a business from scratch, albeit a well-funded business backed and supported by a big multibillion dollar corporation. But, nonetheless, we started from zero. We started without employees. We started without any clients. We started without any suppliers. We didn't even have offices.

As a 21-22-year-old I experienced how a new business is born. This is undeniably a life lesson. A once in a lifetime experience and to do it in a different country, well it's like the cherry on the cake. I had a great boss, Mario Parra. I will be forever grateful to him. Hopefully he reads this because I acknowledge him and I acknowledge his foresight, his trust and the confidence he placed in an inexperienced boy like myself. I was freshly out of college. Hopefully, I added value. But it was certainly a memorable experience for me. We opened up an office in Mexico and we went about hiring employees and buying portfolios. Instead of issuing new loans, the strategy was to grow by acquiring existing ones. We started buying other banks loans. That's how we started obtaining clients. Before we even started knocking on doors and prospecting, we bought clients. So that was pretty interesting to see for the first time. One could grow through acquisition.

But sales had to start and so we went out and knocked on doors and used networking to get in front of CFOs and CEOs of middle and large companies in Mexico. My job description in Mexico was manager of business development. So I had to start knocking on doors and pretty much establishing Associates First Capital in the marketplace. Companies were welcoming the new funding sources. In one of those sales calls, the Mexican prospect company had myself and another person from Bank of America's asset based lending unit do a sales pitch at the same time. We both went in and presented to the CFO and pitched our services and explained why we were a good alternative for their business. The interesting part here was that we didn't do it privately nor did we do it independently. We had to pitch our product and services at the same time in the same room. And to my surprise and utter dismay, I was pitching against the CEO of Bank of America's asset based lending group. Essentially, he was the equivalent to Mario Parra but for Bank of America. So here I am pitching against a seasoned and experienced commercial banker that had been in the commercial banking industry for a very long time. Just my luck! I believe I pitched well. But he certainly pitched a lot better than I did. He had a lot more insight into the prospect than I did. And he was seasoned, I was just starting. He had years of experience and a wealth of knowledge that I didn't have and couldn't even fathom because I never experienced it. But overall, I think I did justice to my company. We did not win the pitch. Bank of America did.

What happened was very unexpected. I got a call a couple of weeks later from a Federico Gonzalez from Bank of America and he said he wanted to meet and talk. Little did I know that he was actually calling me to interview me for a job at Bank of America. When I went to see him, he basically said in a nutshell, *"Arturo I think you did a great job in that sales pitch a few weeks back. I see a lot of talent and I see a lot of potential in you. Obviously you're hungry. I think you would be a great asset for Bank of America."* I was startled. This came from left field. I had no idea that this was ever going to happen. I certainly wasn't planning to change jobs. Changing jobs wasn't even on my radar. You must understand, Bank of America and Associates First Capital are two very different companies. Bank of America is a much bigger company and they offered many other products Associates First Capital could not. And they had a farther and deeper reach. It was an amazing opportunity. For a twenty-three-year-old it was a lucrative job offer. But the potential was more appealing. I was stuck between a rock and a hard place because Associates had given me a priceless opportunity and I felt disloyal just even listening to the offer. And Mario and I had had become very good friends. He had become my mentor. We had a very strong professional and personal relationship. So I went and I told him what transpired. I was upfront and direct. He asked me, *"Arturo are you interested?"* And I said, *"Mario, I would lie to you if I told you if I wasn't, but understand that I didn't look for a job. I wasn't applying for a job. I'm very happy here with you and I'm very happy with the company and I'm very happy with everything we're doing."* He sat me down and I'll never forget it. He said, *"Arturo this is a better opportunity for you. And I would go against my better judgment to hold you back. So go ahead and take it."* I'll be forever grateful to Mario Parra because he was always thinking about me. And he made it a lot easier for me to transition from Associates to Bank of America.

And so now here I am at Bank of America doing pretty much the same thing I was doing with Associates First Capital, but with a broader array of products and services that I was able to offer and with an institution that was far more recognized and had a more established brand and a deeper reach in Mexico. It was one of the biggest banks in the world. I was very much involved in commercial banking from the corporate lending side at Bank of America Mexico. My career went very well and I helped establish Bank of America as a premier lending institution. I was also exposed to the biggest clients across all industries. It was a very enriching couple of years.

But, in my early twenties, I always had the itch to be an entrepreneur. It is a very curious thing in life that most kids whether they're in high school or college, but at a very young age, they have this same itch. We have this voracious ambition to create wealth, to become entrepreneurs. It's so curious and so ironic because it's the worst time we could ever become entrepreneurs. Think about it. What experience do we have? What life or work experience do we really have? What makes us think that we're going to be successful? I mean, we don't have the perspective or the context of how a company is run, let alone run a company. And worse yet, how do you start one? What makes us think that we have that bright idea? Yet we think we have the idea that is going to revolutionize the world. What actually think that we are prepared and will actually revolutionize the world. We really don't know much of anything and the last thing in the world that we actually do have is Experience. Nonetheless, that's the attitude I had and my friends had then. We had this itch that we wanted to be entrepreneurs.

One of my high school friends, a very close friend of mine was in marketing at Procter and Gamble. And another friend of ours was in Guadalajara, Jalisco, in the epicenter of the Tequila capital of the world. We decided to start a tequila brand. We actually started importing a mineral water from Italy. Our friend from Guadalajara started this and invited us. At one of our social reunions that subject came up and we all said let's go for it. Again, Ironic because none of us had any idea how to do this. Not only did we not have a clue, we had no capital. We had no money. We had the "we are prepared and ready to go and no one can stop us" attitude. Looking back, it is the most curious thing.

As a side note, I have always told my brothers my friends, my children that that's the worst thing you can do. I've counseled and advised so many kids that have this this insatiable desire to be entrepreneurs. I tell them to go learn first and gain much needed experience, context and perspective. There will be plenty of time to become an entrepreneur. But they need to understand what it means to have professional dirt in your face and sweat in your eyes and they need to have a couple of scrapes and scars and a few victories in the corporate world before entrepreneurship is right for them. Said another way, *you need to have learned a thing or two about a thing or two* in the professional world. Before you go out there and risk your own professional career, you could be obtaining experiences and getting paid for it. You are not just going to risk your money, what little or a lot of money you may have, but there's a huge opportunity cost in not being in the corporate world learning. In a very good job that's bringing you income and teaching you. The opportunity cost is even bigger than the capital you may invest in this entrepreneur adventure that all these young kids want to embark on. I think there's a time and a place and you need to have experience before you go out there and become an entrepreneur. Experience and life lessons, context and perspective can mitigate a lot of unnecessary mistakes and failures. After some real experience in your arsenal, then go and risk and conquer the world.

Anyway, back to my journey. My friends and I decided we were going to import bottled water from Italy. Our partner in Guadalajara was going to operate it. But before we even got started, another brilliant entrepreneurial idea came to us. Let's start a Tequila company instead. Oh, the young and the restless and the naivety. Anyway, this idea did not just fall from the sky. Our partner was well connected and he knew the owner of an abandoned tequila factory in Atotonilco, Jalisco, about an hour's drive from the city of Guadalajara. Abandoned is an understatement. It had not operated for over 20 years. It was in the middle of the jungle and there were more rocks, plants and trees then actual metal or steel. Trees were literally growing inside the tubing. It was inoperable. However, NAFTA had just been approved and mandated that the United States and Canada recognize Tequila's denomination of origin. The rest of the world followed suit soon thereafter. And furthermore, only 35 factories could actually produce or have a license to produce Tequila. The factories were protected and no other factories could be built at the time. This abandoned plant in the middle of the jungle was one of them. And our partner had negotiated its purchase at cents on the dollar, better yet, cents on the pesos. It was actually genius because we had absolutely no intention, nor capital nor any idea to bringing the factory back to life. I think it was an insurmountable and unfathomable endeavor for anyone. Nonetheless, the genius part was that it gave us a license to fabricate Tequila.

Our partner presented us with this awesome opportunity, or so we thought. Here I am with this voracious desire to become an entrepreneur. And there is my partner who is in marketing and working at Procter and Gamble which is probably the best school for marketing because of all the multiple brands that they own and operate. He was the perfect guy to create a brand, to create a label, to create a name, to create the colors, to create a back story, to create the packaging. We were going to have our own tequila brand.

Of course a lot of planning went into this and I was doing this outside of work. I was working 18 hour days and on the weekends with my friends while I was working full time at Bank of America. We began planning the launch, looking at different bottling alternatives, tasting different tequila types, understanding the tequila industry, and negotiating with different suppliers because even though we had a license to produce tequila, we still needed an operating factory. We had to go to the other operating factories that were actually fabricating tequila and cut a deal with them. And we accomplished that. To this day I am not sure what credibility we had, but we accomplished it. We came up with a product, the packaging and the branding. And this materialized into a prototype. And I thought it was the prettiest bottled tequila I had ever seen. Of courses, it was far from it. But to us young dreamy-eyed entrepreneurs, to receive the first case of 12 bottles of tequila, 500 milliliters of tequila, in a red bottle and a black cork that we had designed, we felt we were on top of the world. It was the first thing we've ever created. We created something from nothing. So the feeling was amazing.

But certainly we hadn't done anything in terms of a business. We had not launched a product, it was not on the shelves. It wasn't anywhere, in any retail store, restaurant or bar. We were light years away from making it a business, a viable business at that. But here we are thinking we were on top of the world. I can't help think about how ironic it is that we were so happy and yet we had done absolutely nothing yet. And the interesting part is, we all decided to leave our jobs and go at this full time. Look out Forbes, here we come.

So I decided to leave a lucrative career at Bank of America to start a tequila company, and needless to say it was an adventure. We immediately rented office space because we had to have infrastructure. Ho naïve we were. Spend first, make money later. Another example of how unprepared we were. Our biggest priority when we got an office was who was going to have the biggest office. We put more value into the size of the office than the actual business itself. In fact, this was the cause of our first real discussion and fight as partners. It just goes to shows how immature we were and how we completely lacked perspective. Here we should be frugal. Here we should put all of our energy and all of our resources into the business. And I'm thinking about if I'm going to get the biggest office or not. And I won't even talk about the furniture, just more of the same.

Life went on. We started the business and we worked hard. We had a very strong partner in our supplier, the factory. He owned four brands and we were subcontracting his factory to produce our tequila, our brand. We had struck a deal with a couple of liquor stores and a few local restaurants. But we were nobody yet. Yet a break came when we struck a distribution deal with a prominent liquor store chain in in Mexico City. We started small. At the beginning, there were little shipments, 20 to 50 boxes a month at most. And we did not start in all their stores, just 2 or 3. It was our responsibility to make sure the product sold. And we did not have the capital. We had to go and promote the sale of tequila and advertise and market it in the stores. In retail, if you put something on the shelf and it doesn't move, the retail store will pull it from the shelfs and put something else that does. They could care less about your product. They'll put something else that moves instead. They're in the business to move products not for them to sit on the shelf.

Even so, I will never forget the first day I was driving by the store and I saw our tequila through the window. I mean, that was one of the proudest moments in my life. We had closed the loop and come full circle. We had started something from zero. We had created a product. And the insane part was that somebody actually validated that product by buying it. It does not in any way mean we were going to be successful. I want to be very clear about this. We were not successful by any means, far from it. So I'm not talking about the exhilaration of success. I'm just talking about the exhilaration that comes from validation that you created something that somebody liked. The retail chain that had bought our product. I went inside and I bought one of these bottles and to this day I still have that bottle. It was a crowning moment in my life.

So guess what we learned very early on in the process that we really hadn't considered: that you need a lot of capital to launch a tequila brand. The naivety. You need inventory. You need to buy the physical bottles. You need to buy the packaging. You need to buy the labels. You need to buy the corks. You need to buy the boxes. And you need to pay the factory for the actual tequila. And you need to put all this together into a finished product that is retail ready. And you need to do all of this long before anybody ever gives you a dime. And then you have to go out there and sell it. You had to pay people to go out and in visit liquor stores and department stores and restaurants and bars and wholesalers. And these guys aren't going to do it for free. And we had our offices and employees working there. For all of this you need capital. None of us had capital. Remember, we were young ambitious broke twenty-four year olds. And so what did I do? What did my partners do? Well, we did what any twenty-four-year-old kid would do. We begged our families. Our biggest supporter was our mothers. We had no money and the little money that we did have was already put it into the business. We raised about a hundred thousand dollars between all of us. That's a lot of money. Little did we know a hundred thousand dollars was a drop in the bucket compared to what it really took to make a successful tequila brand and a viable business around it.

The money helped to buy initial inventory and covered short term expenses. It also helped us buy some much needed media for advertising which is crucial when launching a brand. Remember, we had to make sure those bottles on the retails shelfs were constantly moving. We bought radio spots and more importantly TV spots. And here's where again perspective, context and experience comes into play. We just thought we were going to wander right into the tequila space and knock it out of the park. And none of the big tequila brands such as Jose Cuervo, Herradura or any of the many other well established, five generation brands were going to even look at us. We thought we were just going to stride right into the market and nobody was going to raise an eyebrow. Boy were we wrong. The radio and TV spots we had purchased were very specific. The various channels and time spots were picked to target our specific target market. Whether it was ESPN or MTV or the local channels in Mexico and 3:00 p.m. or 8:00 pm, it was a very specific media campaign that was going to put us on the map. We were certain that we were going to make those bottles fly off the shelves with this marketing campaign.

Long story short, our commercials did not run in anyone of our purchased spots. Rather, our commercials ran between 3:00 and 5:00 in the morning when everyone was asleep, specifically our target market. So what the heck happened??? We had paid for specific spots at specific times on specific dates on specific channels. And none of the commercials ran in anyone of those spots. We ran in channels, times and days that had absolutely nothing to do with our desired audience, or for any liquor or alcoholic beverage for that matter. Our media company broke the news to us: our competition had interfered. The big boys with their influences with the media and the different media outlets ended up rebuying those spots. And because they were very important clients to the various media outlets, the media did not blink in giving them what they wanted. And our budget was a rounding error compared to theirs. That's the way the media works. It's not guaranteed. And that really hurt us. It actually killed us. We had spent most of our capital on this campaign. And we had no idea this could happen and it did happen. And that was how the tequila company started and began its inevitable end. We did make it into some other wholesalers. We did make it into some retailers as I mentioned and some liquor stores. We were a big hit in a particular high end department store. But it was of very little value. We did not have the capital, the connections, and most importantly the experience to really make this a viable business, a long term enduring company. We ended up selling the company to our supplier, to the factory that we had subcontracted the production to. It was a one of the best experiences and yet one of the worst experiences of my life. It taught me so much at such an early age. But I lost money and I lost a dream.

While we were doing this we also started an export business of consumer goods to the Dominican Republic, canned foods actually. We were eager young little entrepreneurs. And we basically jumped pretty much at every opportunity that came our way. This one went well. One of our employees who later became a partner found some good distributors and importers in Santo Domingo, the capital of the Dominican Republic. This was actually a cash flowing business. We made money and the operation was simple. We had one manufacturer in Mexico that we bought from on very good pricing and structural terms and one large importer in the island. We then expanded this to electrical appliances space by importing from Colombia and selling into Mexico. It was basically the reverse of exporting. We used our same infrastructure and know how. We had established strong contacts in the retail space, particularly supermarkets that also sold home appliances. And the Colombian company was a strong manufacturer and that helped in strengthening our credibility. We had good terms with them as well. We ended up selling the export company to a company in the Dominican Republic and shutting down the import company, not because of us, but because our Colombian partner ran into financial difficulties.

Now remember, I was young, ambitious and thoroughly naïve. So I figured I could still do more entrepreneur ventures. Outside of my group, I bought into a discotheque in Mexico City. All for the wrong reasons. The irony of life yet again rears its face. I bought into a nightclub because as a 24-25-year-old I was going out at night and partying like most kids in their early 20s do. And, like everyone our age, you want the best seat and the best table. You want to be with the best crowd. The status symbol of being the owner of a hot club, that was the motivation. No financial analysis, no risk-reward scenario, not even a valuation or an attempt at one. I bought a minority interest in a club because my friend's parents were the owners. And again because ambition at this age has no limits, we decided to take this concept, a success concept in Mexico City and open a new discotheque in Guadalajara. Why Guadalajara? Because we knew a lot of people in Guadalajara because of the tequila business. My partner was from Guadalajara and there was a big expectation for it to come there. The night club catered to the higher end crowd and the higher end crowd in Guadalajara was very familiar with this famous nightclub in Mexico City. But this venture was just between my Guadalajara partner and myself. Now, if you've ever built out a restaurant or built out a bar or build out anything you understand that it is very capital intensive to start these types of businesses. These types of nightclub require more than 10,000 square feet. The remodeling, knocking down walls, creating side by side store fronts into one, the decoration, the sound equipment, the lighting, the bars (there were multiple bars), and many other elements necessary to recreate this night club was very capital intensive. Not to mention the startup costs and working capital; the suppliers of the liquor, beer and wine and the employees and marketing efforts. I sold my percentage in the Mexican night club at a small profit and put up all the money I had saved from my corporate job, literally every penny I had.

The deal was that I was going to put up the initial 50% of the capital requires and my partner was going to put up the remaining 50% in the later stages as he had to liquidate some personal assets. But nothing ever really goes as planned, does it. Two months away from opening I had already put up my 50% and my partner was not able to come up with his. And I lived in Mexico City, hundreds of miles away. It's like living in New York and opening a nightclub in Miami. How was I going to manage this from so far away if partner could not be a part of it, aside from the fact that he had not put up a dime. And mind you I had my other companies that I was already working full time in, the tequila company and the export and import companies. Fortunately, good negotiations and luck reared their good graces. Because there was an anticipation, a "hype" surrounding this new venture as a result if the successful nightclub in Mexico, an investor group was very interested from the onset. We were able to play to that strength and convince a family operated business that owned a couple of restaurants and a 10-year-old nightclub in Guadalajara to buy and invest. I was able to sell 75% of my partner's 50% share and 10% of my shares for not only the needed funds to finish and open the night club, but fully recuperate my investment with a bit of profit before the nightclub even opened the doors. And on top of that, I kept a 40% stake in the ongoing entity. My partner kept 25% of his 50% as earned sweat equity.

And not only that, this new investor/partner had experience and had experienced personnel running businesses they had been running for many years. They were the right operating partner for the job. They believed in the project and they were willing to pay a great price, it just so happened to be a return on my investment. We opened the nightclub and it was a huge success. I made a lot of money. And in hindsight it was a great negotiation on my part, and a win-win scenario for my new partners.

So all these ventures, the tequila company, the import/export businesses, the nightclubs, and even the bottled mineral water company, albeit short-lived, these were my foray into entrepreneurship. And if you can gather from what I've relayed, starting a business is extremely difficult, especially if you don't have experience. You don't know what you don't know. And market research, analysis, or amazing idea on paper rarely makes it into the successes of business startups. There are so many unknown variables. You don't know if the market is going to accept your product, what you have to offer, the service, the experience, or the price point. You don't really know if there is a real need that you are solving. You don't know exactly how your competitors will react. And this is without mentioning the actual operations. We have not discussed managing employees, managing suppliers, managing clients, and managing processes. All of this is hard work in and of itself and you need a skillset, talent and experience to do that. If there's any lesson to be learned at this stage is, as a kid don't start a company and as an adult don't start a company, buy one instead.

Let somebody else take those risks. Let somebody else make those mistakes. Let somebody else fail. Let somebody else sweat and cry and get bloody and get scarred in starting a business and have them put all the pieces in place and make sure that the pieces all work together and that all those pieces now working together begin to turn into sales and sales into profit. And once all that is accomplished and there's some sense of stability and longevity, then and only then do you go in and buy the company. And by doing so you will have mitigated all the risk of starting a company. Now you just have to operate it. The hard work is done. Had I known that then would I have started a club? Would I have started a tequila company? An import/export company? Absolutely not. Because I didn't get an additional reward for the extra risk. For the businesses that did succeed, the profitability was normal, yet the risk of success was enormous. There wasn't compensation for the extra hard work and risk associated with any startup. I mean yes there's a joy to seeing your product on a shelf. There is joy in success. But you can't take that to the bank. That joy does not pay the bills. It doesn't pay for your children's education or your future. And it certainly does not create wealth. Ultimately, let somebody else do heavy lifting and take the risks. And then you come in and you buy the company. This is my philosophy and the reason I have been successful for so many years.

So back to my journey. So at this stage I had lived a very long professional life in a few short years. I was 26 years old and had worked for 2 large companies in 2 different countries and had started or bought into 5 separate business ventures. It was time to reinvest in my education and continue strengthening my Academic foundation. I decide to get a Master's in Business Administration, an MBA. I applied to many schools and was very fortunate to get into the top programs in the USA and two in the United Kingdom. I ended up attending Northwestern University, Kellogg Graduate School of Management. I finished a two-year full time MBA. What a joy it was to be back in the academic world. While extremely challenging, my MBA experienced did not disappoint. I was able to see business in a different light with experience under my belt. I appreciated case studies and theory more, and was able to appreciate my peers' experiences and insights. All in all, my MBA to this date continues to pay dividends.

During the summer between my first year and second year of my MBA, I did a summer internship at Goldman Sachs in New York City, Wall Street, the capital of the world financial markets. I got to see investment banking, mergers and acquisitions, institutional sales and trading activities of equities and bonds and derivatives and national and international shares in companies as well as other financial instruments. I got to see firsthand how the big boys make deals and buy and sell companies. And how to raise capital and how to take companies public through initial public offerings. I got to see a lot thing that I was learning during my MBA and had read about in the media. I was very excited about that. It was a big change from my entrepreneurial endeavors. So when I finished my MBA, I decide to step out of the entrepreneurial world and enter the financial deal making mecca of Wall Street. I went to work for Lehman Brothers. Now, this is 1999 when Lehman Brothers was the lean mean fighting machine of the four big Wall Street firms. Although I had offers for most of the others big Wall Street firms, I wanted to be work with the lean kid on the block. Back then that was Lehman Brothers. I worked in their international sales trading department. And I was there for about a year.

Now during the latter part of my MBA, an Argentinian friend of mine and I had started a business plan regarding logistics in Latin America and using the power of the internet to defragment a very fragmented industry. So while at Lehman Brothers, in my spare time I was helping with that business plan, capital raising and any operational aspects where I could. This was 1999, the height of the DOT.COM boom. We all know how that ended up with the dot.com bubble bursting. But this was two years prior and the space was sizzling hot. Everybody was doing a business plan, launching dot.com businesses, looking to become overnight millionaires. Even the large company were participating, putting a dot.com in their names. Names like AmericanAirlines.com, GeneralElectric.com or GE.com, and Ford.com. And company valuations skyrocketed as a result. I remember when the company Skymall, the magazine that was in all the major Airlines, went from Skymall to Skymall.com, the company's stock price went from something like $4 a share to $18 a share in 1 day. Absolutely crazy times. People who really weren't entrepreneurs were creating the silliest things. Sites like Cats.com, chocolate.com, loveyou.com were popping up everywhere. And while today those domains may mean a lot in value, at the time it was hype and marketing. There weren't any businesses behind them. Yet they were cool names and there was "potential" and these companies would end up raising millions of dollars on a promise, without a business plan or strategic product or service. Again, very crazy times.

My friend from Business School brought on board two other of his friends from Argentina that had a small logistics company. They were in the freight forwarding business. So they knew about cargo, logistics and sending packages. They knew about the ins and outs of the industry. Our business plan revolved around the very same premise that Expedia.com or Travelocity.com or Orbitz.com operate today in the airline industry by defragmenting a fragmented market. If you want to travel from New York to Miami, you would have to choose specific departure and return dates, and an origin and destination. These sites will then give you various different airline providers that serviced those routes and the different prices. Depending on your criteria, travel from point A to Point B, the algorithms will give you pricing information in the desired timeframe. And these sites allow you to choose the best option bringing transparency into the purchasing of airline tickets. They empower the consumer. And remember, these sites did not exist back then or they were in a startup mode. So our value proposition was giving the end user easy and actionable information for sending packages and later sending cargo. So if you wanted to send a package from New York City to Miami, we would show you the logistics providers that serviced that route and their pricing in 24 hours, 48 hours and 72-hour time slots. So you can compare and chose the one that best fits you. But if someone else wants to send a package from Los Angeles, CA to Chicago, IL, the origin and destination has changed and more than likely also the dimensions and weight of the package. So new logistic providers and pricing would be shown based on this new search. In the United States you have four large carriers: you have Federal Express, UPS, DHL and the biggest player which is the United States Postal Service. And it has more than 80% of the market. That's why federal express, DHL and UPS started offering value added services like 24-hour delivery or 48-hour delivery which the United States Postal Service couldn't offer at the time. That is how they would distinguish themselves from the United States Postal Service. So in the USA, this industry is really an oligopoly type of market, with the United States Postal Service dominating the market and only a couple of other players in the industry. It is quite the opposite in Latin America.

The national postal services in Mexico, Argentina, Brazil, Columbia and Chile are very inefficient. They're not well run and are highly bureaucratic and unreliable. So private industry has come in and started fulfilling this need. So much that in Mexico you have over 3,000 companies, in Brazil over 5,000, in Argentina over 2,000 and thousands as well in Chile and Colombia. Compare this to only 5 players in the United States. In all these countries, numerous players/providers create a very fragmented market. In these countries, if someone wanted to send a package or a letter or even cargo from point A to Point B then it's no different than the airline industry having multiple, local, regional and national suppliers. If you have a plethora of shipping options in Latin America in general, it is very difficult for the consumer to know which is the best price or option for sending a package from point A to point B. Our company helped filling this void by offering transparent pricing and options. If a client wanted to send a package from Mexico to Guadalajara and the package weighs one pound our company would instantly show you the various providers and pricing in 24 hours 48 hours and 72-hour time slots. concurrently, if someone wanted to send a package from Monterrey to Tijuana, new providers that served those routes would appear, with pricing relative to the time slots. The value proposition was very similar to what Expedia.com or Travelocity.com or Orbitz.com are doing today in the Arline and car industries. In essence, we were the Expedia.com for the logistics industry in Latin America. And we became the logistics arm to e-commerce store. Imagine any e-commerce store that was selling books or electronics or computers or shoes or whatever they were selling, they had to solve this logistics problem as well. We became their logistics arm just like. E-commerce sites are not in in the business of logistics or payment processing. They are in the business of selling products and services. Just like PayPal eventually powered the payment aspect, we powered the logistics aspect. We also had many clients in the CtoC space like eBay, and the BtoC space like Amazon. This was a very novel idea.

My initial job was also to create a business plan and raise capital from potential investors while I was working at Lehman Brothers. The more we worked on the business plan, met with prospective clients and logistic suppliers, the more we knew we had a winning business solution. I worked hard pitching it to venture capital firms. I visited many in New York City. I started flying to Los Angeles, San Francisco and Buenos Aires, Argentina. And again I was forced to make a decision: to remain at Lehman Brothers or go satisfy the Entrepreneur itch that was again gnawing at me. I left Lehman Brothers to fully devote myself to this new venture. They were very upset and made me give back my sign on bonus, a year after I joined them.

While I was capital raising we launched the Argentinian operation. We started the business on our own, with capital from the four of us. We started hiring employees and building a site for the Argentina market. We were making this a reality. Two of the largest online auction sites, mercadolibre.com and deremate.com, became our clients. And others started signing on as well. These were the Argentinean eBay in 1999 and there were multiple sites. Today they're all consolidated. In fact, eBay ended up buying mercadolibre.com in Latin America. We started in Argentina and our next market conquest was Mexico. While we were opening up this office, amazing news officially arrived. We had a $10 million venture capital offer. We were now entering the big leagues; we were successful enough to raise ten million dollars from venture capitalists. My capital raising efforts had paid off and we were officially funded. Citibank Venture Capital Latin America (CVC Latin America), Merrill Lynch and a smaller venture capital fund out of out of Silicon Valley, Explorador Fund, were the Venture Capitalists. Together they had a 30% equity stake in the company and we, the founders, had the remaining 70%. Although they had veto rights on almost everything minority shareholders. They had veto rights on the use of capital, selling shares or selling the company, hiring key personnel, salaries for us and our top employees, approval of the budget among many other important aspects of the company. This is very common in venture capital and common in private equity although with more flexibility because private equity normally invests in more mature companies. Venture capital by nature invests in riskier ventures and startup companies like ours. Even though they were technically minority shareholders, they controlled the company and we ran the day to day operations.

We now had ten million dollars do accomplish our Latin America roll out. In Latin America, one country alone is nowhere near the size of the United States. So you have to be in multiple countries to achieve the scale you would otherwise achieve in the United States. The business plan called for establishing operations in five different countries. We had already launched Argentina and now Mexico was on the cusp of being launched. Next on the list was Brazil which is the biggest country in Latin America. From there we opened up operations in Chile and then Colombia. Lastly we opened up a smaller office in Miami because Miami was becoming Latin America's Silicon Valley and it was essential to have a presence there. I became the CFO and Business Development. Argentina became our corporate headquarters. I moved to Argentina, although I really lived on an airplane travelling to and from the six different countries we were now present in. It took approximately 6 months to finish the six country geographical roll out. We had hired about 25 people in the Argentina office and probably on average about five to 10 people in each of the other country offices. We had to operate, build and grow this company and ultimately make a profit. To take it to the next phase, we began to get ready for raising an additional round of capital. The goal was to raise $45 million dollars. So we put a new business plan in place and we started the capital raising process led by me.

Citibank, Merrill Lynch and the Explorador fund wanted to participate in the second round to preserve their percentage. But they were very pleased and also helped in the capital raising process by introducing us to partner investors. And so we started the roadshow in Miami. We also flew to Brazil. We had meetings in New York in Mexico and in Silicon

Valley. There was very strong interest. We had a bank out of Brazil that was very interested was wanted to be the lead bank funding this $45 million capital raise. They had lined up two other venture capital firms, alongside Citibank, Merrill Lynch and Explorador fund. We moved through a term sheet and we were looking at legal documents. Almost there. Yet, weeks before funding was to take place, Catastrophe hit.

The dot com bubble burst. Literally overnight, companies began close their doors and go bankrupt. Companies that had raised hundreds of millions of dollars overnight were laying off 100 percent of their staff. And this was not a U.S. phenomenon. It is a worldwide phenomenon. Companies that had 100 million dollar valuations and more in the US, UK, Latin America, Asia began to disappear. The companies that were a couple of months' prior on magazine covers as the next best thing, were now examples of failure. The media headlines were all about tragedy and doom. Billions of dollars were lost by investors, institutional investors, private equity funds and venture capitalists. Now, we all know what happened. It was the big dot com bubble bursting in 2001 and 2002. And it killed a lot of companies, many of which never should have lived. But good companies as well as bad companies went bankrupt. And the debacle almost destroyed the internet industry. Our business was obviously affected. But we had a real business model and we had a real offering and a real need was being solved. We were providing a real service. We were giving customers a transparent way of seeing pricing based on their logistic needs. Because we were a real company, we survived. We had to preserve the cash we had as we were in survival mode.

Most of our clients were disappearing because they were auction sites, e-commerce or other Internet. Over 90% of our clients and our pipeline disappeared. We were smart and we adapted quickly. We started hiring salespeople and traded the Internet site with computers. And these salespeople with computers were now visiting non internet companies and offering logistic services. We evolved into a freight forwarding company. And although we survived, the business model was radically altered. We were forced to close the Chile, Colombia and Miami operations because scalability was no longer an option. The Mexico operations was bought by the Mexican country manager. And we ended up selling the major company, the Argentinian and Brazil operations to a Brazilian company. We still had money in the bank from the $10 million we had raised. So with both these sales plus the cash, we were able to preserve our investors capital and make them whole. They did not lose money which in the context of the situation was an enormous triumph. While most investors were losing all their money, we preserved 100% of their investment. Needless to say we did not raise the additional $45 million dollars.

Creating this company and living this experience was a very different then my previous entrepreneurial adventures. It's not every day you get to start a company on a brand new technological platform, raise $10 million dollars from renowned financial institutions, grow the company in six countries, manage an international company, only to unwind everything and sell it in pieces, all in the span of 2 years. People don't experience this in a lifetime, what I experienced in a fraction of a lifetime. As I thought about what do I do know, I reflected on this. We had just raised millions of dollars. We created an international company in six different countries and we were on the verge of raising $45 million more. And then it just disappeared overnight. So trust me when I say it is very difficult for me to really understand what my next step was going to be.

I wanted to be an entrepreneur. But I had just build a multimillion dollar international company. Anything I did as an entrepreneur was going to pale in comparison to this. On the flip side, I did not want to go back to corporate America. I had just left corporate America approximately 2 years prior. How do I go back to a corporate job and report to someone else and be tied down to specific duties after this amazing journey? It seemed that any corporate job was just not going to be interesting or fulfilling. So again I was stuck between a rock and a hard place. I knew I had to take a break from business, but a vacation or a sabbatical was never an option. So I decided to go and invest in myself. I decided to go back to school to immerse myself in academia and strengthen aspects that I believed needed strengthening. I decided to get another graduate degree, another Master's degree. In fact, I ended up getting two.

I did a double Master's degree back in Boston University, coincidentally. I received a Master's degree in International Relations and also in Communications. I had just launched this international company in 6 different countries and I realized how important communications was. How do you launch a new brand? How do you achieve optimal public relations? What is the best business development strategy? Communications is not necessarily just about marketing and advertising. It's also about understanding the media, understanding branding, understanding your audience on a local and on a mass scale. Doing business in six different countries is very different. It is not the same to do business in Argentina, in Mexico or in Brazil, Columbia, and Chile for that matter. You deal with different laws, different cultures, different regulations, different customs and in general a different more localized form of doing business. And one does not naturally know how to operate this. So I thought understanding history, understanding international relations international business, different foreign currencies, different markets, different risks different political ties, different diplomatic ties all play a role, directly or indirectly, in any business venture. I did a joint master's graduate program in International Relations and communications at Boston University as a result of all this. And to my delight, part of it was actually administered in London.

This was a beautiful time in my life. I obtained two Master's degree that certainly complemented my professional experience. I lived in Boston and was able to live in London. I also met my wife. While at Boston University we were engaged. We have been happily married going on 15 years strong. So it was a great time, really incomparable.

After graduating, we moved to Miami where I was involved in a Panamanian telecommunications company. We built a telecommunications processing data center in Panama by buying a building that was part of a former military base in that country. Panama is a geographic central hub for telecommunications where all the fiber optics linking Latin America and the United States meet. We started a company to do data management, data storage and data processing in Panama City called a NAP or Network Access Point. It also serves as a redundant access point for big financial institutions and big corporations. I was involved in raising capital and operating it. This company was funded by a Spanish consortium and eventually sold to a large Panamanian company in the telecommunications space.

We decided to move yet again. We moved to Mexico as my wife was pregnant. All of my family lived in Mexico at that time and I wanted my children to be surrounded by their grandparents and their uncles and aunts and cousins. I grew up with my extended family ever-present and family to me is the most important thing in life. I did not want to derive my children of this. So we decided to move back to Mexico. Upon arriving, I was offered a job at KPMG Mexico as Managing Director, in charge of launching their mergers and acquisitions division from the ground up.

KPMG Mexico was very strong in valuation services, financial advisory on distressed assets, loan portfolios, restructuring companies and helping companies perform due diligence for targets they wanted to acquire. This is the Financial Advisory Services Division within the company. However, they weren't involved in the actual transaction of their clients. They were not a Mergers and Acquisition shop in Mexico. Yet KPMG around the world does a lot of merger and acquisition advisory services. They are very strong in middle markets in helping companies buy and sell companies and also raise capital via private equity or venture capital. I was hired to start this division from scratch, backed by a wealth of experience that surrounds KPMG's financial advisory services and KPMG as a whole. This was an amazing undertaking and opportunity. I was able to start a division form the ground up and in the mergers and acquisition and capital raising space. We began very strong and immediately started receiving mandates and doing multiple deals. We helped company's buy businesses and helped company's position themselves to be sold and guided them through the entire process. We also helped companies raise capital. Complementing this was a high degree of valuation analysis and financial advisory was needed. We were constantly valuing targets and also valuing comparable companies. Together with this came the need to value distressed assets, intangible assets, and international assets. My business valuation skills went into expert mode. I knew how to value companies before but now I was actually taking classes from KPMG, the experts in business valuations, and learning very sophisticated and complex valuation techniques and methodologies. We did over 40 deals and must have valued over 75 local, national and international companies while I was at the helm. A couple of years into this, with evolving professional success, I had to abruptly leave and move to the United States.

It's important to mention that while I was in KPMG starting this new division, I was also giving classes at the graduate and undergraduate level at a university in Mexico. At the undergraduate level, I was giving classes in financial administration. So essentially, this is basically an introduction to the capital markets, to investment portfolios, to capital budgeting, to cash flow, project risk, cost of capital, capital structures and dividend policy. At the graduate level, I was giving classes in corporate finance, similar to financial administration, but in more depth. We looked at mergers and acquisitions, valuation, securities analysis, the cost of capital as well as many other topics. A second class I gave was investment evaluation; in essence how to analyze various investment opportunities. There are many underlying topics as the previous 2 classes. For example, I taught valuation, risk management, cost of capital. But I also taught quantitative and qualitative fundamental analysis, financial modeling, financial indifference points among other topics. Teaching was me giving back to the community.

I love to teach and I was teaching undergraduate students, which are very different than graduate students. Undergraduates want to get out of your class very fast. They are there because they have to be there. Learning social skills were more important to them. The challenge was making it interesting for. Making the material relatable so I used many practical examples from my professional experience and many case studies. The graduate level was a different playing field. This was a different type of student. These students were paying to be there. Some were attending at night as they had full time jobs. They wanted to get an MBA, they want to learn. Some had specific projects; whether they were a startup, operating a company or they're working in a company where there were deficiencies they want to find answers to. A graduate degree was also a means of enhancing their professional career. So they were very involved.

I was invited to partake in various business ventures. I became a board of director for two or three of the companies. One venture in particular was in the business of building and operating facilities for the third age or senior living. These were senior living facilities where they are apartments that operate more like a hotel with activities. And although very nice, they have medical facilities onsite and architecturally built to address the aging process. It was a business model that caters to people that can no longer live in a big home but still want to live and have amenities and have like-minded friends and activities so they can be socially awake and active. They have trips and field trips to the city and around the country, and pools, and movie theaters, and library, and sports facilities but they also have medical attention. The rooms were beautiful little apartments with medical apparatuses inside such as emergency buttons so a nurse can come and ramps as opposed to stairs with railways. It's a model where you are promoting life yet attending people that are in their later years of their life. This was a project in Mexico where we were able to build and operate three of these facilities in three different cities that housed over 900 people. I did not make any equity investments into these facilities. I was invited by one of my students to help in the operations and the startup phase and everything that went into the funding of this company. And I received sweat equity as a result.

I wanted to teach because I value academics. One learns a lot from the daily interaction with students, experienced or inexperienced. They will challenge you, they will challenge theory, they will challenge a lot of things you hold to be true through your business and real life experiences. One has a chance to research and understand the newest trends, the newest tools, and the best practices in the various facets of running a business and investing. I am a strong believer that as a business professional you should always have one foot in academia learning theory, the latest trends, newer technologies and newer processes. This allows one to be constantly evolving beyond the confines of their business reality.

The mindset of many business owners we target to buy businesses are people are stuck in their ways and life and business has probably surpassed them. One of the reasons why they're frustrated and their business may not be growing as fast as they could be is because they have fallen behind. They have not stayed on top of the new technologies, the new trends, the new developments, best practices. And this leads to stagnation and stagnation kills the soul, it kills the mind and it does not let you evolve, create, and grow. I believe one always needs to be in touch with education, with academia. You learn things and it challenges you to learn things and to validate what you think you know and what you do know and what you're doing every single day. Academics has been a big part of my life. And it's been a great counterbalance to my professional career and a big part of my success.

Before we moved back to the United States, I also was involved in an entrepreneurial venture while I was at KMPG. I had started a real estate brokerage company in Mexico. We grew it to 25 realtors. This proved to be a very successful real estate company. We're made a lot of money selling homes in Mexico. We were also selling investments in the United States in the preconstruction/predevelopment phase. We were focused primarily in Miami and some investments in Las Vegas. We sold these developments to real estate investors. They would put 20% down while the buildings were being built. And when the building was finished they would sell that to the end user through what's called a simultaneous closing without having to put down the additional 80%. These were multimillion dollar apartments and condominiums, for the most part. The investors were making over 100% return on their investments. I personally had five investments in different preconstruction projects and made well over 100% on my investments. It was a very lucrative time. In conjunction we were buying and selling residences in Mexico. As the broker, I only had the expenses of the office and marketing and advertising activities. All the realtors were on commissions. It was a very low expense business venture and as deals came in and we closed on homes, the company became very profitable. I started that business and I was running it while I was at KPMG. Though I was very involved in launching it and guide the strategy, I was absentee owner from a day to day operations. The business essentially ran itself. I had good management in place. I sold the company to the management team. When we moved to the Unites States.

It was 2007 and Mexico was undergoing terrible security situations. The government had a frontal war with the drug cartels and it was spilling into main street. My family and I were held up at gun point on numerous occasions. It was far too dangerous and I was not going to continue to expose my family to this, in spite of the success of my professional career. In 2007, we moved back to the United States. Our second daughter had recently been born. So I was now a father of two beautiful girls, a 3 year-old and 1 ½ year-old. I used my contacts in Miami and they introduced me to a medium sized Texas an oil and gas company that was doing fracking before fracking was as well-known as it is today. They had a vanguard fracking technology and they had a lot of assets in the form of oil and gas reserves. It was run by a management team and a board of directors that were very seasoned and experienced, at least it seemed so on paper. The president and chairman of the board was a former president of Occidental Petroleum, a multibillion dollar oil and gas company. He was also former president Lyndon B. Johnson's chief of staff. This is an older gentleman. He was in his early 80s or late 70s when I joined this company. The board members were friends of his. They weren't as active as they were in earlier times in their professional careers. On paper this company appeared to be backed by former CEOs and CFOs of a large multibillion dollar gas companies. This seemed very enticing. I invested in this company and I became the CFO. Little did I know what I was getting myself into.

As I mentioned, the company looked amazing on paper. It looked like a first class company given the fact that management had heavy experience in oil and gas at the president, chairman and at the board of director's level. And they presented this well. They also had strong oil and gas reserves However, as I started diving into their financials I began to see the true picture, it was not pretty. I started to detect a lot of let's just say, shady stuff. To give you an example, the company had reserves valued at roughly a $65 million dollars. Yet on the Income Statement they had about $4 million in revenue and were spending $9.5 million dollars in expenses. They were losing $8 million a year. The vast majority of that $9.5 million dollars was going to salaries. They had a team of about 25 or 30 people that were getting top notch salaries. And the three main officers, the CEO, the CFO and then the CIO (this is an oil and gas company so why do you need a chief information officer?), were making each well over $350 thousand each. Between three people, that's over a million dollars in spending. Mind you, there was only $4 million in revenue and there were another 35 people there that were making $100 thousand, $150 thousand, and $200 hundred thousand in salaries.

Not to mention that the offices were situated in a prime location paying high rental rates. Their offices had custom furniture which must costs anywhere between $35-$40 thousand per office and they had maybe 10 private offices. That is crazy money on decorating the office. And this is an oil and gas company that was doing just $4 million in revenue. Oil and gas companies don't tend to receive clients so do not need fancy furniture or prime office location. These guys were visiting investors across the USA, always traveling first class. It seems their spending habits were certainly not reflective of a $4 million revenue company but more akin to a $100 million revenue company a profitable and a profitable company at that, which this company certainly was not. As I got deeper into the finances and the operations of this company I could not understand what the other 35 employees actually doing. Not to mention, there were another 12 employees in the fields. They were working and working hard in keeping that revenue coming in. But at the office, they had land men on salary, geologists on salary, finance personnel on salary and numerous administrative assistants. In this industry, most if not of all of this is outsourced and only used when needed, not permanent on salary. And the chairman of the board, this high profile individual, was also making $350,000 dollars a year, but doing absolutely nothing. He would come to work mid-morning, sit in his office for about three hours and then go home. He was never involved in the operations. He never once went to the fields or speak to the personnel out in the field, or ever talked to any prospective investors. He was completely hands off and was basically "milking" the company.

I was in a company that was bleeding cash with incredulous cash management. The way they had been addressing this millionaire deficit was by raising capital through individual investors. I invested $650 thousand myself with my family and I thought that money was going to increase revenue by being applied directly to production as I was told. But far from it, was going to bridge that gap between income and expenses and pay those outrageous and unrealistic salaries and extra personnel. And they have been doing this with multiple investors for a very long time. In fact, there were over 450 individual investors and actually one private equity fund out of Russia. The money wasn't getting to the fields so the fields were not being developed and the oil and gas wells weren't producing. It was a terribly run company with the wrong kind of management and Board.

The company had also taken on far too much debt. They had raised a lot of money via debt from investors that didn't want to take equity in the company. They took convertible debt and hands there was there was about 35 million dollars in convertible debt that this company had also raised across the past four years. And the fund was owed another $30 million so there was over $65 million in debt. So not only did they have an expense problem they had a debt problem as well. Little by little I started reengineering the company and ended up achieving a full financial and operational overhaul. I implemented a deep cost structuring of the company and began terminating people, people that had no business being there. And the first people that were terminated were the CFO and the Chief Information officer. To this day I have no idea what a Chief Information Officer does for a little small oil and gas company. We terminated 90% of the 35 odd people in the office. We did not do much in terms of terminations with field personnel as they were vital for operations, real operations.

From the debt side, I had to go out and talk to a lot of investors and convince them to convert their convertible debt into equity as the debt load was making the company financially unviable. We were able to convince all individual investors due to the extreme financial restructuring we were implementing. We were left with the $30 million debt owed to the Russian fund. We sold a couple of the oil and gas assets and reserves that were in California and with the proceeds substantially reduced the debt with the fund. After these divestitures, the company was left with assets in Kentucky, New Mexico and Louisiana. We brought the debt down from $65 million dollars to about $9 million dollars. We took the overhead down from $9.5 million dollars to under $3 million dollars. The company was now cash flow positive and making a profit. The investors, I believe for the first in a long time, were happy and saw a real future. They could actually see a return on their investment in the horizon.

The company still had chairman of the board, a former Occidental Petroleum CEO and all the members of the board of directors were also friends, cronies of this guy. And the company still had a CEO. And he was the real culprit behind the money investing scheme. He was always talking to the individual investors. He talked a great game. He seemed to understand oil and gas. But he was not an oil and gas man. He simply could never increase production. And that was his number one responsibility. So he was always out collecting money from investors to fill the deficit. The company had not progress from an operational standpoint for years. Later I discovered that he had been barred by the SEC, the Securities and Exchange Commission, from a previous oil and gas company that he worked at for an SEC violation because of the same capital raising practices he was employing at this company. And then this is where it became even more interesting. Because of all the fund raising efforts this person had done, we had crossed the 500 investor level and by regulation had to become an SEC compliant company, one which would prohibit him from working at because of his SEC violation. Fortunately, without much convincing, he stepped down as CEO.

The Securities Exchange Commission has a rule that if there were more than 500 investors in a company you have to become an SEC compliant company, no different than a company that trades on the New York stock exchange. To be an SEC compliant company means significant financial reporting requirements and audited financial statements for your company, among many other filing requirements. Essentially you have to let the public know everything about your company in a transparent way. Any significant event, hiring a key employee, strong production from a well, a significant discovery, new debt, among other relevant events had to be filed with the SEC and available to the public at large. You are now considered a public entity by the Securities and Exchange Commission. And you have to start filing 10Ks in 10Qs, the annual and quarterly audited financial statements with all the relevant notes.

We had become a public company but not a publicly traded company. So we were no different than an Apple, General Electric or IBM in its reporting requirements. We just didn't have shares trading on any stock market. We had all the filing requirements and associated costs, but absolutely no benefit. This is what happens when you do not plan your fund raising activities correctly. We were bearing all the costs of being a public company. The natural conclusion was let's become a publicly traded company and give our shareholders liquidity and use all the benefits of being a publicly traded company such as issuing shares to the public and raising funds in the financial markets. We did was is commonly known as an initial public offering an IPO. It is a bit different than a traditional IPO. We became publicly traded by doing what is called a Form 10 SCC filing and then issuing shares to the public. Nonetheless, the end result was the same, to start trading on the Stock Exchange. This was my first time I had taken a company that I owned, was managing and operating and made it a publically traded company. We now had the proper vehicle to raise money and make this a very successful company.

To better position ourselves, we went out and hired an experienced oil and gas expert through an executive recruitment firm. He had worked for Amoco for approximately 30 years and then he went out and started his own company with $18,000 and grew that company to over $34 million dollars in value and sold it. He then went into retirement. Yet, he wanted to come out of retirement and was impressed with the financial turnaround and saw real potential in the oil and gas reserves. He saw this as a wonderful opportunity.

But the first thing he told me was that chairman of the board and that board of directors has to be terminated because as he put it, *they are sucking the money out of this company and they added zero value.* So we met with the private equity fund and devised a full corporate takeover to get rid of the board of directors and ultimately the Chairman of the board. We had to perform a complete, text-book corporate takeover. To do this we had to convince the majority of the individual investors, and do so in secrecy. We laid out a plan to run a real oil and gas company that was going to increase production, revenue and hence create real vale. The investors were fed up at this stage as they had been in this company for many years and had not seen any returns. They happily obliged. We called an extraordinary shareholder meeting and had a proxy fight to fire the chairman of the board and the board of directors and install a new board of directors. At this point I had only seen this maneuver in movies and here we were doing a proxy fight to take full control of the company. We were able to achieve this with a resounding 73 percent majority which is almost unheard of.

We suddenly had a clean slate. We could take the company where it should have been taken all along. We had a strong cost structure. Our revenues were more than our expenses and we were cash flowing. The company was profitable. We had cleaned the balance sheet and shrunk the debt down to about $4 million dollars, which was very manageable. And we had fields producing. We now had to raise money and invest it into the fields to increase production and thereby increase revenue and create value. We had a seasoned CEO that immediately understood oil and gas assets, devise a development plan to develop these fields, to develop these wells and a drilling and production plan so we could produce oil and gas. The oil and gas industry is a highly capital intensive industry so you need to raise money to accomplish your development and production plans. Oil rigs and drilling equipment is expensive.

So with the financial re-engineering, the corporate restructuring, the overhaul of the board of directors, a real development and production plan in place and the stock as a currency, we were ready to raise capital. We held many presentations in New York with different funds, banks, and investors. We had strong momentum, there was great interest and we had great traction. And then the unthinkable happened in 2008.

I remember landing on a Friday after widely successful meetings in New York to the rumors of Lehman Brothers possibly collapsing and Fannie Mae and Freddie Mac were not far behind. The mortgage markets were very weak. Bear Stearns, a seasoned investment bank on Wall Street, had gone bankrupt a couple of months back. And so there was a lot of anxiety and nervousness in the markets and in Wall Street in general. We did not pay much attention because we were in Oil and Gas industry, not in the mortgage industry. I remember arriving from New York after having many successful meetings. We were ready to raise approximately $60 million from various different funds and float additional share in the market. We were a publicly traded company and we could sell our shares to institutions and them in turn sell them to their retail clients. Knight Capital was our underwriter and market maker, alongside many other funds and institutional investors. We were weeks away from raising $60 million and implementing an aggressive oil and gas development and production plan that was going to deliver tremendous value to all shareholders. But I'll never forget that Friday. I landed and I saw the news that Lehman Brothers may on the verge of going bankrupt. I didn't think much of it at that at that time as it was Friday. But over the weekend the worst case scenario emerged. One could read all over the news, all over the papers, the rumors that something was going wrong with Lehman Brothers. It was like a pot with water boiling slowly boiling over.

That Sunday evening, Lehman Brothers declared bankruptcy. We all know what happened next, the financial crisis of 2008. Although at the time, no one had any idea that this was the beginning of what we all know is to be one of the worst financial crises in US and world history. What began in the mortgage industry quickly spread and permeated all related and unrelated industries in the United States and worldwide. The world went into one of the deepest recessions and what's been called something close to the Great Depression of the 1930s and 1940s. Real estate plummeted, multibillion dollar companies went bankrupt, industries went bankrupt, even countries went bankrupt. The biggest bailout in in U.S. and European history was implemented. Over $500 billion dollars to bail all aspects of the world was put into effect.

On the oil and gas front, oil prices plummeted. Before the recession, oil was at $147 a barrel. It went from 147 to 130, 120, 110, 100 to 90 then to 80 dollars a barrel. We could not see the end in sight. And every time it broke what we thought was an impenetrable floor threshold, it dropped again. Within a few short months, oil prices went from $147 dollars all the way down to $30 dollars. All of our financial projections were now garbage because they were all based on a conservative $110 dollars a barrel. Imagine that. That was at the time very conservative. The worst part of all this was that all of our financial prospects, all of these investors that were going to buy our shares and invest in the company were now in deep financial problems of their own. The whole world was in problems. There was no credit. No one investing. The capital markets came to a grinding standstill.

Investors had margin calls. They saw their portfolios go from $10 million to $2 million and had millions of dollars in margin, debt collateralized by the securities. When value of their portfolio fell below their debt limit, they were forced to sell their shares to meet the margin calls and pay the debt. And that created a vicious downward spiral cycle. And this was happening to millions of people around the world. Our shareholder base and the prospective investors that we had visited in the past couple of months were all in these type of situations. Banks stopped lending. Banks actually didn't know if they themselves were viable, if they were going to survive. They all had problems in their loan portfolios. Retail investors were scared as the stock markets lost double digit percentage points day in day out. It was a scary time. Nobody was lending and nobody was investing. Our funding sources to raise capital disappeared overnight. We went from having so much momentum to no momentum at all. We kept up a good fight. We kept seeing investors. We ventured forward. But what we slowly began to realize was that this was going to be longer than anyone really understood or expected. This was not a temporary correction but a permanent change. This was a worldwide phenomenon and it was deep. Most people didn't understand the extent of it. In hindsight, this went on for many years. Not until 2012-2013 did one begin to see a bounce back.

Oil is a commodity. One cannot control prices. Our $4 to $5 million in revenue went down precipitously because oil prices went down. Our revenue went down by more than 70%. Now we were losing money again. But you can only slim down a company so much. You still have to pay the rent, you have to pay people in the fields, you have equipment out there and it has to be maintained. We still had drilling costs and subcontractors to develop these fields and drill the wells so we could produce oil and gas. So without money we were not going to produce. And there was no way of getting money from the financial markets, let alone our investor base.

We had to survive. We started trimming down even more. We sold oil and gas assets. The CEO and myself did not take a salary for over 6 months. We went from 6 people to 3. Eventually, there was no real need to have a CFO. So I decided to step down as CFO and stayed on as a board member. I sold my shares in the open market months before so I was financially stable.

But what a roller coaster ride. Talk about peaks and valleys and peaks and valleys. I did more as a CFO in this small oil and gas company then a CFO does in a multibillion dollar company his entire career. I financially restructured the company and made it profitable. I restructured millions of dollars' worth of debt and made it viable. We did a managerial cleanup and a corporate takeover through a proxy fight. I took the company public on the US Stock market. And we made the company survive during one of the worst financial crisis in modern history. I did this all in the span of about two and a half years. What an incredible experience.

So here I was again with this question: what do I do next? While I was mulling this over in a short, "semi-sabbatical", I thought about the small business space. But it was a very bad time. You did not know whether the deal you were analyzing would survive the next day due to the harsh financial times. Companies were suffering and the economy was extremely shaky. It was a very uncertain time to do deals and to buy companies. I didn't want to rush into anything. Nonetheless, I started further analyzing the small business space given everything that I had learned. I had started many businesses. I had bought businesses and sold businesses. I had invested in businesses big and small, national and international. I had raised millions of dollars. I had done corporate takeovers. And I had taken a company public. I had launched products from scratch. I had many successes and a couple of failures. I had plenty of experience underneath my belt. I was seasoned.

I had always looked at small businesses throughout these past 15 years. I would always look at businesses to buy. I was always analyzing small business profiles sent to me by business brokers or through the internet. I would analyze the financials. I would analyze the industry. I would analyze the longevity of the companies and who was managing them. But I never really pulled the trigger. I did realize that this was a very liquid space. The small business acquisition space was very active and liquid. There were many businesses for sale just like homes, just like the real estate market is a very liquid market. There were many businesses out there that one could buy at any given time, just like residential real estate. And there were many companies willing to finance the purchase of those businesses. There's a whole infrastructure around real estate market that makes buying real estate extremely easy. That same phenomenon is prevalent in the small business space. That exact same mentality and infrastructure surrounds small business. There are numerous banking institutions, investors, and loan programs out there that help you buy companies like there are in real estate. And I saw this and understood that this was a great opportunity. I had just never pulled the trigger.

I realized that this was very straightforward and easy. And I began looking at all industries, not just the ones that were in my comfort zone. As an entrepreneur, I had already been involved in various different industries that I knew little about before I entered them. Before I got into the oil and gas company, I didn't know anything about oil and gas. Or logistics, or tequila, or exporting and importing, or real estate brokerage, or all the other industries I had been involved in buying and selling businesses. I came to the conclusion that maybe I should buy small businesses instead of starting them. What an epiphany!!! And that's exactly what I did.

The first thing I did was go through a business broker. Of all the sourcing options to find small businesses, a business broker is the last place to buy a business. I did not fully understand this back then. Using a business broker, we ended up buying two businesses, an Italian restaurant and a live music country western bar, both within 3 days of one another. This was now 2009.

The bar had been open for over nine years. It was a stable business that had a stable brand in a stable market with a loyal clientele and strong employee base in place. The same was true with the restaurant, only the restaurant had been opened for 5 years. There was good management and good systems in place. We bought both companies with owner financing. In fact, the bar turned out to be a 100 percent financed deal. We also bought the real estate with the bar and it was financed by a local bank for 90% of the real estate value. The restaurant was not a 100% owner financed deal because I didn't necessarily know that you could do 100% financing back then. In hindsight, I would have done that deal differently. I would have had 60% owner financing of the purchase price and I would have used the business assets to finance the remaining 40%. There was enough restaurant equipment to accomplish this, not to mention stable sales for merchant cash advances or inventory financing. But the bar was financed 100% without any equity down. I still own the bar to this day and it is a cash flowing business. Both were great investments and both were owner absentee run business. So, from day one I saw that light.

The bar was a million-dollar purchase including the real estate. And the restaurant was more than a million-dollar revenue business. These are my first deals in the small business space. And they were great. We were very hands off, by design. We weren't in the business but controlling the business. We were managing the strategy part of it. We did get involved in the administration part just so we could understand the restaurant and bar space. But all in all the managers ran the day to day operations. So I could go on vacation and nothing would happen. And keep in mind, these are two businesses that I had no experience in. This is a clear example of how you don't need have to have experience to buy businesses.

Since then I ended up buying two more restaurants in the hamburger space that were in distress. And then I bought a real estate brokerage. I bought them without putting any of my money with owner financing and asset based lending. I have bought additional restaurants, a pest control company, an ecommerce company, a financial services firm, a web advertising company an Internet marketing company, a meat distribution company, a bakery, a steel fabrication plant, a food distribution company, a remodeling company, a loan brokering company among 30 other types of businesses since buying the restaurant and the bar in 2009. And the count is ongoing as I am active in the business buying space to this day and for the foreseeable future.

And my professional journey continues...

About the Author

Arturo has been an entrepreneur, a sought after consultant/coach and public speaker for over 25 years. He has been involved in well over 130 business purchases and business deals.

He has successfully started, bought and or sold over 45 national and international companies, personally from his own portfolio, primarily in the small business space. In some cases, with operating partners. He has bought restaurants, started a tequila company, a consumer goods export company, a technology company, bars and night clubs, a pest control company, fast food restaurants, real estate brokerages, a steel fabrication company, franchises, a wholesale distributor, a Data Center, a loan servicing company, a logistics company, an import and distributor of electrical appliances, an oil and gas company, a theater production, a professional soccer game, a senior living management company, among others. These have all been done for his own portfolio and in many cases without using his own capital.

He has raised money from angel investors. He has raised millions of dollars from venture capital funds like Merrill Lynch Venture Capital, CVC Latin America, Citibank's venture capital arm as well as Explorador fund in Silicon Valley. He has taken a company public on the stock market in the United States. He has also been involved in corporate takeovers as an entrepreneur. He has raised millions of dollars from banks, asset based lending institutions and angel investors. All of this for his portfolio companies previously mentioned.

He has worked at Goldman Sachs, Bank of America, Lehman Brother, and KPMG as managing director of their mergers and acquisitions division where he was involved in over 90 deals.

As a professor he has taught courses in *Investment Analysis, Corporate Finance and Capital Administration* at the graduate and undergraduate level.

He holds a Masters of Business Administration from the Kellogg Graduate School of Management at Northwestern University and a Double Masters in International Relations and Communications from Boston University.

To receive updates, special offers and future products please sign up at:

www.arturohenriquezauthor.com

www.ingramcontent.com/pod-product-compliance
Lightning Source LLC
Chambersburg PA
CBHW051332220526
45468CB00004B/1607